Ethereum

How to Safely Create Stable and Long-Term Passive Income by Investing in Ethereum

Introduction

Other than setting records, Ether is a valuable cryptocurrency with a lot of potential in the next years – with an industrial and intrinsic value.

Among the chapters that you will find in this book are:
- An Introduction to Ether & Ethereum
- Concerns about Investing in Ethereum
- Understanding the Ethereum Architecture
- Ethereum's Entrepreneurial Ecosystem

Furthermore, this book will fill you in on all the essentials about Ethereum. If you're hesitant about investing the Ethereum platform, the information inside will hopefully help clarify matters for you. And you're also be able to discover and understand how to SAFELY invest in Ethereum – in a step-by-step manner.

If you're bothered by concerns that it's too late to invest in Ether and the Ethereum platform, know that it's not.

It's not too late, and in fact, it's rather early to invest in Ether since it hasn't even come near mainstream adoption unlike other cryptocurrencies (e.g. Bitcoin and Litecoin). JP Morgan, Microsoft, Samsung, and Intel are just but a few Fortune 500 companies that are in the process of exploring Ethereum. And since it hasn't reached its maximum growth capacity yet, it is continuing to grow exponentially.

According to analysts who calculated its value (using astronomical analyst systems and calculus in a complex method called *Gann Square*), Ether was seen with a 5000% increase just within a year. And it still has plenty of potential to grow even further.

And thus, this is one of the best points where it would be ideal take advantage of Ether's current price. Based on Ether's transaction growth chart, its price will keep on increasing. So, allotting money on

Ether and the Ethereum platform, then committing to hold the position for several years, is likely a financially rewarding move.

Chapter 1 - Ethereum: The Future of Digital Payments

In 2013, a man named Vitalik Buterin was looking at a lineup of science fiction elements. Then, a particular word seemed to sound more interesting than the rest. It captured his interest since it contains another word (Ether) that he fancies.

This word was Ethereum, and this man became the founder of a blockchain-based platform, as well as a high-potential cryptocurrency.

What Is Ethereum?

Ethereum, based on blockchain technology, is an open platform that grants the authority to build (then deploy) over a *Dapp* (or a decentralized application) to developers. With a hash rate value (at its peak) of 3 TeraHash (or 3,010 GH per second), it has a large infrastructure. Its developers, led by Vitalik Buterin with assistance from Charles Hoskinson, Anthony Di Lorio, and Mihai Alisie, designed it for high-end GPUs (or Graphics Processing Units).

And since it runs on blockchain networks, it also comes with the advantages of decentralized networks such as:

- 0% downtime, or the inability of apps to be switched off or go down
- Security, or the protection against fraudulent activities
- Immutability, or the inability of a 3rd party to modify data

Initially, the Ethereum platform's distribution was done via a public blockchain network -- in an ICO (or Initial Coin Offering) form. During which, about 35,000 Bitcoins were exchanged for about 60,000,000. This allowed almost USD $14,000,000 to be raised, which, consequently garnered 14% of supply.

Furthermore, Ethereum's distribution continues to be done via a public blockchain network. And this public blockchain network works alongside the distribution of the Ethereum platform's cryptocurrency tokens called *Ether* (with code ETH).

User Accounts

In the Ethereum platform, a blockchain features blocks of various sizes. Alongside, there are various types of user accounts that come with 20-byte addresses.

The two types of accounts are as follows:

- #1: External accounts – accounts with private keys
- #2: Contract accounts – accounts with contract codes

The primary difference between the two types of accounts is in the authority that controls them. For external accounts, the control is assigned to human users, which consequently pass control to external accounts.

On the other hand, contract accounts are not controlled by human users. Rather, these accounts are controlled by internal codes. While they can use contract accounts, humans would need external accounts to activate contract accounts.

Furthermore, contract accounts are allowed to perform an operation if instructed by external accounts. So, unless prompted by external accounts, these contract accounts cannot perform native operations (e.g. API calls and Random Number Generation).

Smart Contracts

The Ethereum platform's notable feature is the use of scripting functionality called *Smart Contracts*. This enables users to create tokens that are compatible with exchanges and wallets under a standard coin API. More importantly, this means that it is able to facilitate the exchange of valuables (e.g. money, stocks, and property).

And thus, with Smart Contracts, you can expect a self-operating program that executes orders automatically once conditions are met. Since their operations are done via a blockchain network, they execute according to the original programming – without the possibility of downtime, censorship, and 3rd party interference.

Here's an overview of a Smart Contract's operations:

- First, a code (based on an option contact) is written into the blockchain network. Despite the contact serving as the public ledger, this code is written with the protection of anonymity of the involved parties.

- Then, a Smart Contract is executed once a trigger (e.g. strike prices and expiration periods) is hit.

- Lastly, since a Smart Contract was run, regulators begin inspecting market activity by using the blockchain technology. However, throughout the inspection, regulators are obliged to ensure privacy (of the involved parties).

Chapter 2 - Concerns about Investing in Ethereum

Apart from the #1 common concern of whether it's too late, investing in the Ethereum platform can seem worrisome due to the general perception that Ether is "too volatile". While its price is predicted to increase, Ether can still move vigorously. Thus, if a currency is perceived to be too volatile, it is against the sage advice of avoiding that currency.

On the other hand, while it is part of the equation, the highly volatile nature of Ether is not usually a disadvantage. If there are no changes in price, profitability is virtually non-existent, too. Sure, investors could experience a huge profit loss. However, a huge gain in profit is also a possibility. And despite price fluctuations, returns will still be produced.

Criticism Linking ETH to Ponzi Schemes

Both Ethereum and Ether have been subjected to criticisms due to talks of enabling *Ponzi schemes*, which is an illegal investment operation. Since Ethereum operates via a decentralized system, it's not uncommon for scammers and other fraudulent investors to exist. Thus, these fraudulent investors can take advantage of Ethereum users (especially the non-specialists).

These Ponzi schemes are considered illegal since their system doesn't involve legitimate businesses. These schemes are not upfront about their agendum of monetizing from new recruits. Instead of enabling every member to profit according to their effort, these schemes are designed to allow older members to profit.

Take, for instance, the event that concluded in the jailing of (at least) 15 representatives and the seizure of more than USD $2,000,000 in investor funds from a Mumbai-based company called OneCoin. After its pitch of being a new version of

Bitcoin, OneCoin was busted by financial enforcement officers.

On the other hand, both Ethereum and Ether are far from being part of Ponzi schemes. So long as an individual doesn't commit to different hierarchical groups, and they remain independent Ethereum users, investing in Ethereum poses no such danger.

Risks of Investing in Ethereum

Just like an investment with other cryptocurrencies in other blockchain platforms, a top disadvantage of investing in the Ethereum platform is the risk of centralization. The purpose of distributed cryptocurrencies gets defeated. Since large amounts of Ether are held by certain entities [e.g. The DAO (or Decentralized Autonomous Organization) Hacker], there are risks that these two entities will join forces and begin disregarding Ethereum's decentralized system.

Should these two entities join forces while the Ethereum platform is still under the PoW blockchain? This means that these large stockholders can tremendously influence Ethereum's operations, and they can affect other network participants. With their authority and extensive control, these large stockholders can create rules and oblige other network participants to adhere to such rules.

On the other hand, the Ethereum platform is shifting to the PoS blockchain (as mentioned in Chapter 1). Under the PoS blockchain, the aforementioned security threat is eliminated since the rule of PoS states that 51% (at least) of the stock should be acquired by an entity before changes could be declared.

While it seems acceptable, the scenario is a virtual impossibility. Acquiring 51% of ETH would mean buying 51% of all ETH, which can sum up to almost $5,000,000,000. And even if a said entity is willing to put in USD $5,000,000,000, the scenario is virtually impossible in relation to ETH's limited amount in circulation.

Apart from this, here are other risks associated with Ethereum:

- Unless 100% necessary, relying on the Ethereum platform solely for critical apps is not recommended.
- Ethereum does not provide a stable source when it comes to value (according to Vlad Zamfir, a top Ethereum developer).

More about the Proof of Stake Blockchain in ETH Mining

While the PoS blockchain is relatively more secure than the PoW blockchain, Casper (or the PoS protocol) is also a major threat to Ethereum mining operations. Since it follows a different execution order than what miners are accustomed to, its unique consensus algorithm can render force hashing obsolete. Consequently, it will affect profitability.

Thus, a solution is to construct a GPU setup that does not rely solely on a single network. For one, it's considerable to make the switch from the PoS blockchain to GNT (or Golem Network Token).

Ethereum's Entrepreneurial Ecosystem & the EEA

If you're doubtful of Ethereum's capability of leading you towards a promising financial state, perhaps, it's best to hear the advice of experts in digital currencies.

One prominent digital currency expert has acknowledged the potential of the Ethereum platform. He said that, just like other cryptocurrencies, Ether can open massive opportunities for different financial groups. And unlike other cryptocurrencies, a striking advantage that the Ethereum platform has is its optimization especially for developers and software engineers. This expert happens to be a blockchain investor by the name of William Mougayar.

Furthermore, he states that Ether is a hit mainly since many developers and software engineers adopted Ethereum. These people are also willing to participate to witness its progress.

For instance, recall that market crash in June 2017. From USD $319, ETH fell to USD $0.10, which consequently resulted to many ETH traders losing a big sum of money. But within seconds, the crash was rectified, and Ether's price rebounded.

And as mentioned previously, many companies that belong to the Fortune 500 group are one with the Ethereum platform's journey to success. And apart from the many Fortune 500 companies, many research groups and blockchain startups believe in Ethereum as well. Consequently, these communities united to form the EEA (or Enterprise Ethereum Alliance).

By May of 2017, the EEA had 116 members. Other than JP Morgan, Microsoft, Samsung, and Intel, the other enterprise members are:

- Cornell University Research Group
- Merck KGaA
- Toyota Research Institute
- Banco Santander
- Accenture

Furthermore, it is the EEA's purpose to coordinate the engineering aspect of open-source reference standards, as well as private permissioned versions of Ethereum. The condition is that the members are mandated to work with the Ethereum developers addressing the common interests in particular fields such as:

- Consulting
- Management
- Banking

- Health
- Pharmaceutical
- Technology
- Automotive
- Mobile
- Entertainment

Ethereum's Biggest Impact

The biggest impact of Ethereum may lie in the fact that while it addresses fast-growing sharing economy, it continues to accommodate the traditional economic system. So, while it caters to the users who prefer more modern approaches to furthering entrepreneurial ventures (e.g. using computers and mobile devices), it does not ignore the characteristics of traditional economies (e.g. production is based on needs, tribe/family-centered, reliance on barter).

More importantly, the incorporation of both the modern approaches and the traditional economies makes Ethereum ideal for both the younger and the older generations. So, an individual – regardless of rapid or old-fashioned way – can leverage the Ethereum platform for his/her entrepreneurial goals.

Chapter 3 - Understanding the Ethereum Architecture

The DAO (or Decentralized Autonomous Organization, as mentioned earlier) is a demonstration of Ethereum's impressive architecture.

It was in 2016 when The DAO, a leaderless project on the Ethereum platform, was able to raise about USD $50,000,000 worth of Ethers. Its seamless operation can be traced to the creator of The DAO framework, Christoph Jentzsch; The DAO's design is to operate as a load of smart contracts.

Thus, the collection of smart contracts equates to by-laws that grants voting rights to any entity with The DAO tokens. More importantly, any entity with The DAO tokens can allocate resources, which in turn, generates a range of returns.

While it was exploited in June of the same year, it was forked 3 times in the last quarter of 2016. Consequently, the Ethereum platform features a debloated blockchain, an increase in DDoS (or Distributed Denial of Service) protection, and a preventive measure against spam attacks.

And after realizing The DAO's success, members of the Ethereum community were optimistic, of course!

Ether

In the Ethereum platform, Ether is used for all kinds of services (e.g. computations and payment of transaction fees. Since 2016, it was attributed to the 2nd largest market cap among all other cryptocurrencies. And since 2016 to the first quarter of 2017, its value spiked to almost USD $7,000,000,000!

Here is a list of facts about Ether:

- Ether is known for fluctuations in trading volume. In March 2017, the 24-hour trading activity in the Ethereum platform rose to about USD $600,000,000. And this number (also based on a 24-hour trading activity) does not even cross the USD $100,000 line. Overall, however, a gradual uptrend is observable with Ether.
- Over-the-Counter Ether trading is offered.
- Due to the Ethereum platform's flexible design, developers are granted permission to issue assets beyond participation on the blockchain network.

Performance of Blockchains

And as far as performance is concerned, the Ethereum platform's performance is laudable. Transactions are handled fast – in fact, much faster compared to other platforms. And since they are less likely to get delayed, transactions (even multiple ones) tend to proceed without errors. Plus, there are barely any investors that have reported complaints due to the platform's performance.

On top of that, the Ethereum platform's impressive nature can be traced to its permission for trade-offs. This means that not only a single type of blockchain is allowed. So, should they opt for private and permissioned blockchains or public blockchains, Ether users do not have to worry about incompatibility issues.

Here are some considerations:

- Private blockchains do not mandate the use of internal tokens whose value is set by open markets. Consequently, both reporting and regulatory obligations are reducible.
- Private blockchains are relatively cheap in terms of maintenance.
- Private blockchains require identification of participants via either a designated gatekeeper or a group consensus.

- Private blockchains focus on the pursuit of legal action, and rely less on incentives (internal). Its focus is on identified participants both at the application and network level.
- Public blockchains are relatively effective when it comes to resisting censorship.
- Public blockchains can provide relatively strong evidences of events.
- Public blockchains can provide higher security for relatively small apps.

Programming Language

Regardless of a preferred type of blockchain, many Ether users are also impressed at the Ethereum platform's Smart Contract feature. This is due to the comprehensive and high-level programming nature of Smart Contracts.

Smart Contracts use abstractions and necessitate an idealized (and usually, well-defined) instructions from the programmer. And beyond establishing a complex level of programming, their design revolves around suppressing complex information beyond the present level.

Furthermore, Smart Contracts' ability to function exceptionally reveals the multiple programming languages that it can accommodate. Some of the usable programming languages are:

- Mutan – a deprecated Go-based programming language
- LLL – stands for Low-Level Lisp programming language
- Serpent – a Python-derived programming language
- Solidity – composed of a library of languages (such as JavaScript and C)

The EVM's Role

With Smart Contracts come the EVM (or Ethereum Virtual Machine). In the Ethereum Yellow Paper, the EVM is formally defined, and there, it is referred to as the runtime environment for Smart Contracts.

Simply put, the EVM serves as the heart of the Ethereum platform. As mentioned, Ethereum can run programs that were created using multiple programming languages – both of arbitrary algorithmic simplicity and complexity. And this is due to the EVM's flexible design.

Ethereum Mining: The Dagger Hashimoto Algorithm

Also behind the Ethereum platform's impressive performance is the Dagger Hashimoto Algorithm (or the algorithm proposed for Ethereum). This algorithm was designed to meet three goals. These are:

> · Light client verifiability, or the need for a block to be verified as efficient by light clients.

- Full chain storage, or the storage space requirement for mining during the full blockchain state, and even with the possibility of pruning using particular contracts.

- ASIC-resistance (or Application-Specific Integrated Circuit Resistance), or the mandate that grants marginal profitability to ETH miners who are using ordinary computers with spare power (CPU).

Furthermore, the Dagger Hashimoto Algorithm can execute orders well since it was constructed using two previous work pieces.

The first piece is an algorithm that Vitalik Buterin himself created, *Dagger*. This algorithm incorporates acrylic graphs to achieve both memory-easy validation and memory-hard computation. However, while it was chosen to be a substitute solely for memory-hard algorithms (e.g. Scrypt and Balloon Hashing), it was proven to come with vulnerabilities to hardware acceleration (shared memory).

Thus, the Dagger algorithm can be more efficient with another winning algorithm that works on its vulnerabilities. This algorithm is *Hashimoto*, created by Thaddeus Dryja. Apart from working on vulnerabilities to hardware acceleration, it uses memory reads, and lets these serve as the limiting factors during the mining process.

And since it is a progressive platform, the Ethereum platform acknowledges the need for revisions regarding the Dagger Hashimoto Algorithm.

The Best GPUs for ETH Mining

On top of this is the significant role GPUs play. Since not all of them are created equally, GPUs must be chosen accordingly to maximize profitability when mining in the Ethereum platform. And while it's true that those GPUs with higher power exists, not all high-power GPUs are more efficient than their low-power counterparts.

Thus, when choosing GPUs, it's best to consider some factors such as:

- The delivery of Ethereum hash rate should be high, and its power consumption should be low.
- It should feature power target tuning.
- It should feature memory clock.

Chapter 4 - Ethereum vs. Blockchain

While Ethereum and Bitcoin are both powered by the concept of public ledgers and protected by cryptography, these two are different in many ways, especially in the technological aspect. For instance, Ethereum is coded using the Turning complete programming language, while Bitcoin's code runs on stack based language. Other noticeable differences include block time (Bitcoin transactions are confirmed in minutes compared to seconds in Ethereum) as well as their fundamental builds (Bitcoin uses SHA-256 hash algorithm, while Ethereum uses ethash).

But in general, Ethereum and Bitcoin greatly vary in purpose. While Ethereum is developed as a platform that facilitates P2P contracts and application through its own currency medium, Bitcoin is developed as an alternative to fiat currency and so a medium of payment and a means to store value. Even though both Ether and Bitcoin are cryptocurrencies, the main purpose of Ether is not to provide an alternative way of payment but to facilitate then monetize the works done in Ethereum, so developers could build and operate distributed apps.

While it is like Bitcoin and other blockchain networks, Ethereum's outstanding difference is its primary purpose and capability. Other blockchain networks are used for monitoring the ownership of currencies. Meanwhile, Ethereum's primary focus is on the execution of Dapp's programming code or on blockchain development's technical aspect – no more, no less.

Apart from that, these are the other ways that Ethereum can differ from other blockchain networks:

- While other blockchain networks support cryptocurrencies that are virtual equivalents of gold coins, Ethereum functions similarly to a world computer.

- Ethereum is a platform that supports multiple applications – both secure and decentralized applications.

- Ethereum works with the PoW (or Proof of Work) blockchain. However, shifting to a PoS (or Proof of Stake) blockchain is in the process.

- Ethereum's scripting language goes beyond C++; it is constructed in Turin-complete scripts, which consists of Python, Haskell, Java, JavaScript, Go, Rust, and C++.

- Ethereum carries out transactions relatively fast. While other blockchain networks have a block time of minutes (for example, Bitcoin's block time is 10 minutes), Ethereum's block time is only (about) 12 seconds.

- Ethereum users are less likely motivated by various ideologies (e.g. free market and individuality), and have an indefinite aversion toward a centralized system (e.g. government and major financial institutions).

- Other blockchain networks' design do not allow scalability. Meanwhile, Ethereum's design allows infinite scalability since it uses block gas limits (e.g. complexity needs, storage needs, and bandwidth usage) for every transaction's cost.

While it is crucial to know the difference between Ethereum and Bitcoin in technical terms, it is more important for you, as an investor, to know which one is a better investment.

Remember, any form of investment comes with its inherent risk, and when it comes to the investment considerations for digital currencies like Ethereum and Bitcoin, the rewards and risks are the deal breakers.

Bitcoin has experienced a surge in increasing value in the last five years. Even though the price fluctuates, the long-term movement is mostly upward. As of this writing, its price has peaked at

$3000, before plummeting to almost $2000, then rising again.

Similarly, Ether also experienced a more significant rise this year, moving from $20 to more than $400 before plummeting to $10 and then bouncing back upwards only in a span of several hours in Q2.

While it is exciting to witness the fluctuation of these digital currencies, it shows high volatility that places the reward/risk ratio of digital currencies somehow at par with playing in a casino or betting on a horse race.

Bitcoin is at a better position right now as there are retailers and companies that are already accepting payments through BTC. This gives Bitcoin the credibility as a payment method for goods and services in the future. It naturally takes some time for any new technology to become famous enough to be accepted in the society. Emails and fax machines were useless until enough people began using them. Bitcoin is becoming useful, because the number people who are using it is increasing.

It is also relatively easy to acquire Bitcoin. More people are now familiar or have experienced using digital wallets, which makes the market bullish. Aside from surviving controversies, its value appreciation is also becoming more stable.

But on the other side, Bitcoin is still mysterious. No one is in control of the platform, and no one has even seen its creator Satoshi Nakamoto. Moreover, those who are forming the cabal that administers the Bitcoin blockchain are diverse, and are not always in agreement. Hence, for long term investors, Bitcoin could still be too precocious and too virtual.

The general market sense with Bitcoin is that without any market intervention or damaging attack, its value shall continue to rise to the levels, which could even surpass the current price of

$3,000. And experts believe that this could happen a lot sooner than expected.

The important milestone to watch out is the moment that the 21 millionth BTC is mined, which will all turn into a corner. The platform shall become finite and the service charges could be defined by then.

Financial experts believe that Ether is a better product than Bitcoin. Even though it is very volatile because of its age, it has two promising features.

First, its creator Vitalik Buterin is an actual person who is active in the development of Ethereum. Similar to Steve Jobs or Elon Musk, he serves as the image of Ethereum, and has authority in speaking about its development, which includes its vulnerabilities. Factors such as these that are very tangible usually reassure the market.

Second, Ether - as a digital currency - is only a part of a greater platform that is still in development -

The Ethereum. As a smart contract platform that runs on the blockchain technology, Ethereum also has a better chance to become integrated in the future global economy. Major economies such as the UK and China are now on the works to embrace blockchain technologies, and it is expected that every industry that depends on transactions (which virtually means all industries) will likely to use blockchain, particularly Ethereum into their business practices.

Both Bitcoin and Ether are promising investments at their current standing. But we may never know what the future may bring.

Considerations that may complicate the choice between Ethereum and Bitcoin may largely involve their relative early phases that signify a relative immaturity of the platform and administrative policies. Even the best programmers in the world today may not be able to predict random elements as well as the vulnerability from cyber-attacks.

Moreover, you must also take note that these blockchain technologies are all running on electricity as well as computing power. Bitcoin and Ether can be expensive to mine. Even though they in general bring hope for the future of financial transactions, there are a lot of vulnerabilities. Countries with access to affordable electricity, cheap labor, and wide access to computer networks may take the lead in mining digital currencies, and this, too should be considered by long-term investors.

At present, both Ether and Bitcoin are great investments that you can put your money for fun, and if you can tolerate the risk of high volatility.

Chapter 5 - Step 1: Know if Ethereum Is the Right Investment for You

Before we explore the factors that will guide you towards your Ethereum investment goals, it is important first to understand the difference between investing and trading. Even if you have prior knowledge to this basic concept, I still encourage you to read this chapter so you will have a refresher and gain insight through the lens of cryptocurrency.

In general, trading and investing are two different strategies to make profit in the financial markets. The main purpose of investing is to grow wealth over a long-term by buying and holding a portfolio of bonds, stocks, funds, and other available financial instruments.

As an investor, you can normally increase your profit through compounding or when you reinvest your profits into more shares or units. Your investments are often held for a particular period of time that may range from months to years, or even decades. You may also take advantage of the perks that are involved in investments like interest and dividends.

Like other traditional markets, the price of Ethereum also fluctuates. But as an investor, you may ride out the risk with the expectation that the price will surge again and any loss will be restored. In investing, you have to consult market fundamentals to look for investments such as price/earning ratios or management forecasts.

Meanwhile, trading involves the higher frequency of buying and selling financial instruments such as currency pairs (forex), stocks, or commodities. The main purpose of trading is to generate the profits, which could outperform investments. When you are an active trader, you may choose to target at least 10% monthly profit in comparison to the 10% profit of an investor after a long term. Trading profits are usually made by purchasing instruments when the price is low then sell them at a higher price at a shorter period of time such as weeks, days, or even minutes. On the other hand, traders can also make profits by selling units when the price is high then purchasing more to cover when the price plummets. This is known as short in the market, which means you can still make profits even if the market is crashing.

Investors are often trained to be patient and pass on less profitable positions. Traders, on the other hand, are trained to take profits or losses within a shorter period of time. Stop loss orders are used by traders to automatically manage the losing positions at a fixed price. Traders are also skilled in using tools for technical analysis such as moving averages and stochastic oscillators to look for the trading setups with high yield profits.

In Ethereum exchange, you could make profits through trading or investing digital currencies. If you want to invest, you are more likely to look for higher returns over a longer period by buying and then holding Ether. Meanwhile, if you want to trade, you may likely take advantage of the rising and falling markets so you can make regular profits.

Hopefully, you now have learned the basic difference between investing and trading, and you are now ready to explore the various factors that could help you in your decision whether Ethereum is the best investment for you today.

Why Invest in Ethereum?

Investing in Ethereum can be a lucrative activity regardless of your experience in the financial markets. This instrument is fairly young, highly volatile, and has wide spreads at the moment. Arbitrage and margin trading are also now very popular, so most people can still make money in investing in cryptocurrencies.

46

The high volatility and some instances of meltdowns in the DAO platform has probably done more to attract more investors as well as traders than any other digital currencies including Bitcoin. Every projected crash of digital currencies including Ether just builds hype for the market that makes it more popular. The publicity causes the price of Ether to increase because more traders and investors are becoming aware and interested.

To a layman, Ether may be perceived as a digital gold rush - a future venture that anyone can do anywhere and anytime. But, the reality is this: many investors give up in cryptocurrencies after only investing several months or when they experience a market meltdown. Unknown to them, this is the nature of digital currencies. They come with high volatility and the price may extremely fluctuate, sometimes in a matter of minutes.

But this doesn't mean you should let go of the opportunity to become an early participant of what is regarded as the future of money. The takeaway point is that you must first be educated on the nature of Ether - its similarities to conventional financial commodities and its uniqueness as a digital currency.

When Ethereum was introduced, it was phenomenal because it was seen as a better version of Bitcoin, which is a popular cryptocurrency on its own. But only after a few years, Ether has become only one, even though among the most popular, of the hundreds of digital currencies that are running on blockchain and encryption.

Like Bitcoin, Ether has the advantage of a decentralized platform, so you don't need a third-party to act as a middle man or a central entity to administer the transfer. Therefore, it is possible to send value to anyone regardless of their time zone or location that eliminates the need for traditional organizations such as wire transfer companies or banks. Also, Ethereum helps businesses and organizations to fulfill obligations and be paid for their work through the Ethereum network without the complexities of the existing business models.

All Ether transactions that have ever happened are recorded in a public ledger that is also based on the blockchain technology. This ledger allows any member of the Ethereum network to review the records. Therefore, it is extremely difficult to defraud the system.

But despite its benefits, there are still uncertainties if Ethereum will be widely embraced in the future and entirely replace the common transactions that we are using today. However, it is clear that we are now at the dawn of a revolution that we may make substantial profits from. After all, the concept of money and the banking system used to be an innovation thousands of years ago, and it has changed the world.

What Is So Special about Ethereum?

Ethereum is one-of-a-kind because of the innovative idea of being free from any single entity as well as the technology used to run it. It has a promising good start, but before you begin investing in Ethereum, you should understand first some things about its nature.

Ether Can Be Used Around the World

Take note that Ether is not a fiat currency, so its price is not affected directly by the economy where you live or the policies of a specific state or a government. Similar to Bitcoin, Ether had some roller-coaster ups and downs before it attracted investors, and many of them are linked with worldwide events. For instance, the sudden price increase of Ether in 2013 was connected to the banking crisis in Cyprus. The government has implemented strict banking policies, so access to cash was limited. Hence, there was an increased interest in finding alternatives to store value and pay for goods and services other than traditional currencies.

Ether, alongside Bitcoin and LiteCoin, was among the best alternatives during the crisis as thousands have decided to reinvest their wealth and stop losing value over their fiat currency. Nonetheless, there is no single person or authority could control Ether.

Ether Has High Volatility

Ether became famous because of its fast and frequent price fluctuations that can occur several times in a day. This is an enticing trait for traders who like to make fast profits, but a disadvantage for investors who are interested in making compound profits.

You Can Trade Ether Anytime

Take note that there is no official platform to trade or exchange Ether. Hence, there is no fixed price for this digital currency. Unlike stock market and the forex market, which have certain operating hours, you can still trade Ether anytime even if it is on a holiday or Sunday night. Many of the trades are within the same price range, but there are also some potential to make profit when you try to arbitrage. And based on historical data, Ether can really surprise you with the price fluctuations.

Investing Vs. Trading Ether

There is a considerable difference between investing and trading Ether - similar to conventional financial markets - investing money on stocks is quite different if you trade on forex. But when you invest in Ether, you can learn more about purchasing digital currencies.

It is fairly easy to purchase Ether, which largely depends on the exchange and wallet you prefer. But this is nothing like purchasing foreign money when you are abroad. This is an easy thing to do. You just need to find the right exchange, wallet, then trade

Ether. Therefore, buying Ether is common among people who would just like to try the digital currency then invest a portion of it, or for those who are curious about it, as a new virtual commodity.

Meanwhile, investing is a long-term strategy that requires maintaining your portfolio that contains different digital currencies, conventional hedge funds, and business perspectives. Basically, those who are investing in Ethereum are not looking into the volatility of the market and they are usually not interested in giving up their investment during price fluctuations.

Trading Ether on the other hand is often part of a short-term strategy. You may try this new digital currency, watch how you can trade for a few weeks or months, then sell your Ether when you think it is the right time to sell. Hence, those who are trading Ether must be sensitive to price fluctuations and may need to respond immediately to become profitable.

What Are the Risks in Trading Ether?

Even though there are inherent risks associated in both investing and trading Ether, the latter carries more risk because of the dynamic nature of this digital currency. If you like to be an investor, you have to learn how you can survive extreme price fluctuations. Hence, you must have backup resources to help you stay in the game despite of a possible meltdown.

Meanwhile, Ethereum traders are often more akin to gamblers, because they have to immediately react to market conditions fast enough to make a profit or stop losing their money. They must also be skilled enough to determine if it is the right time to call the game. Most of the risks in trading in digital currencies, even in conventional markets are normally related to the errors of untrained traders such as putting all of their investments or money in one market.

Of course, if you really want to invest in Ethereum or trade Ether, you need enough money that you can use to make substantial gains in the market. Like any other investment, you must be wary and only invest in secure and reliable wallet. Take note that no one is administering the exchange, hence there is always the possibility that the platform will close. Yes, Ethereum is a modern platform to make money, but the classic wisdom in investment still applies - don't put all your eggs in one basket.

Capital Risk in Investing in Ethereum

If Ethereum has caught your attention as a viable investment, there is a big chance that you have some experience trading or investing with conventional financial markets first such as stocks or forex. If this is the case, then you are probably aware that you should only use a safe percentage of your capital in one trade. During the initial phase of your investments, you first need to experience and understand the digital currency markets.

But unfortunately, many beginners are often disoriented with the prospect of how much they can make from trading Ether. It is true that compared to the stocks and forex, Ether is a more vibrant commodity and you can really make a lot of money during extreme fluctuations. However, this also carries higher risk. The price movement of fiat currency can be measured in small percentages of a dollar. But in the case of Ethereum, the rates could rise and fall on extreme conditions several times per day.

Is it a Good Idea to Trade or Invest in Ether?

There is no one-size-fits-all answer for this question, as the most ideal option for your case will rely on your level of education in this new commodity as well as the resources available at your disposal. You may choose to invest in Ether from a minimal amount, which you can keep on growing as time passes by and as you gain more knowledge and experience. Ethereum trading is also a long-term strategy that may result for you to gain a substantial amount in the future.

Meanwhile, trading is recommended for those who are more sensitive to the depth and nature of virtual currencies and those who have the courage and excess money for trade. The regular fluctuation of Ether can be a valuable experience for any trader, but it could also result to substantial loss.

Chapter 6 - Step 2: Familiarize Yourself with Proven Investment Strategies for Ethereum

Investing in Ethereum has its own sets of risks and rewards. More and more people are enticed to try Ethereum because it has shown a surge in median price over the previous years and shows great potential for the future. Most of these investors are venture capitalists who are interested to make profits out of financial technology commodities such as Ether.

Is Ethereum a Lucrative Investment?

Fintech experts believe that cryptocurrencies like Bitcoin and Ether are on its way for their peak, and those who ride on the trend early on can gain substantial rewards. This is in spite of the fact that it does not yet have the same convenience and value of fiat currency. But with the fast development of blockchain technologies and smart contracts, it is safe to say that this virtual currency will become more common in the future.

Establish Your Own Investment Plan

The best way to make sure that you make profit from your Ethereum investment is to have a plan. Accumulating wealth through your digital currency portfolio will provide you varied results when you invest in stocks or forex. Because the price of Ether may significantly fluctuate depending on the market demand, it is important that you establish a clear goal with practical and realistic values so you can decide if you want to invest or trade Ethereum instead. Hence, establishing a plan will help you a lot to make sure that your investment in Ethereum will be profitable and worthwhile.

Be Prepared for Price Fluctuations

It is common for Ether price to fluctuate several times a day. As an investor, you have to understand the common reasons behind the fluctuation. Take note that Ethereum is an independent platform on its own, and Ether is used as an alternative currency within the platform. This makes traditional regulation policy not applicable, and different nations have the prerogative to support or not support Ethereum. Ether is also vulnerable to bad news and rumors, because the price is closely related to the demand, and any form of bad publicity could have an effect of Ether's total value in the market.

You Can Mine Your Own Ether

It is possible to generate your own Ether if you choose to start your mining efforts. The first thing you have to consider is the cost of electricity and the initial equipment you need to purchase. Since there is also a range of equipment that you can use to mine Ether, it is possible to earn substantial income with this option. Moreover, there are now groups that are beginning to combine their efforts in order to mine digital currencies such as Bitcoins and Ether, and although many of them are not formal companies, they are becoming large players in the mining efforts. If you are interested in Ether mining, the ideal strategy is to set up your base in an area where maintenance expenses will be minimal such as countries with sustainable and renewable energy.

Strategies in Ethereum Investing

If you are not yet ready to invest in Ether, you can start observing the market as a P2P exchanger. You have to join a P2P exchange marketplace like Bitsquare or LocalBitcoins, so you can offer a service in your area to trade Ether. Adding a spread will ensure your profitability. For example, you could offer to buy 2% below the market price or sell 2% above the price of Ether. People will be happy to pay your spread if you can offer convenient ways for them to deal with you. You may include personalized deals or you can make sure that you are always available to offer your service.

However, you may need to make some deals first by responding to online ads for people who are looking for P2P Ether before you can ask for the spread. This will allow you to gain enough reputation and credibility in the niche to earn customer trust.

The good thing about being an Ether exchanger is that you don't need to study comprehensive financial analysis to become one. This is the main reason why this is the ideal way to start investing in Ethereum. Becoming a digital currency investor will require you to have more skills and knowledge. Meanwhile, traders often use online exchangers and usually aim to buy or sell depending on whether they are expecting for the price to rise or fall.

If you wish to become a trader, you may choose to provide a service, by filling out the order books with offers that can be taken up by people who like to trade digital currencies. But take note that the main purpose here is not more on customer service, but simply to take offers as a form of bet if the Ether price will rise or fall.

You may still make profits as an exchanger regardless if the price is rising or falling as long as the market is not fluctuating too fast. Moreover, if the market is rising, then it is best to buy more, by offering a better buying price and average selling price, or focus on purchasing. Therefore, as an exchanger, you could increase your profits by becoming a trader, while offering trading services will provide you a better way to test the market and sharpen your skills.

Another way to make small yet regular profits is by making offers rather than taking them. Once you place offers into the order books rather than accepting offers that are already placed, you can possibly gain a better price. Because you are also providing a service - you become the market maker, which allows the exchange platform to serve as a trader without the need to gain large amounts of your own capital by integrating your own liquidity.

There are also exchanges that are offering rewards when you make offers rather than taking them. These rewards could be in the form of lower trading fees, or even Ether incentives and bonuses. By becoming an exchanger, you can closely watch the trend of Ether rise or fall, which is a fundamental lesson you have to learn for long-term investment.

A well-established strategy is crucial to become successful in Ethereum investing. You have to know specifically what you want when you are opening a trade - your target profit before you can build up before taking it as well as your breaking point on the loss you can withstand. It is also important to determine what time period you are working on and what form of change will drive you to revisit your strategy.

Following the Ethereum Trend

In the stock and forex markets, the price rates are usually for long term. The whole price movement will be in one direction for several years or even months at a time. A clear trend will be consistent even if there are price fluctuations. Experienced market investors often look for this long-term trend and may place their investments for the trend.

As an investor, there is actually no need for you to distinguish the point at which the trend will turn and a new trend will begin against the previous trend. It does not matter if it may take you at least six months to verify a trend if the average trend in a certain market takes a year to settle.

Fundamental Analysis in Ethereum Investing

If you have tried to invest in stock market, you are surely familiar with fundamental analysis, which you can also use in trading or investing digital currencies such as Ethereum.

In general, fundamental analysis will require you to look at the fundamental data, which could affect the price of the digital currency. This includes the volume reported by individuals and organizations that are currently using Ethereum, the number of Ether transactions every day, number of wallets against the number of active wallets, and many more. This data can help you project what is the actual value of Ether now. Your decision will also rely on whether you think Ether is undervalued or overvalued and then you can trade or invest according to your assumptions.

Even though fundamental analysis is a popular tool used by investors to assess the different asset classes like equities and fiat currencies, some experts believe that this strategy can be more complicated if you use in digital currencies.

For instance, it is easy to assess the stock of a company. You just need to look at certain items on the company's balance sheet, then decide whether it is worth its value or not. But in the case of

Ethereum, you cannot assess its earnings or revenue.

Therefore, it can be a challenge to obtain an accurate valuation for Ethereum if you refer to its future cash flows in a manner similar to the valuation of other assets such as Amazon stocks. In response, investors on virtual currencies are now using fundamental analysis based on some new set of metrics.

Even though Ether is considered as a new form of asset class alongside Bitcoin, the same rules could be used for conventional currencies in the forex market. Moreover, all the economic theories and laws can also affect cryptocurrencies. Hence, the starting point for all fundamental analysis should be the demand and supply of the currency, which can affect the prices.

The Role of Demand in Evaluating Ether

There are several factors that affect the demand of Ether, which includes actual trading, adoption, and transactions. Investment experts highlight the essence of user adoption, which is important to the long-term sustainability of the currency. In terms of what is driving the user adoption, Ether as a currency can have different uses. In general, fiat currencies are used for exchange of goods and services, a unit of account, or for value storage. Beyond the DAO platform, Ether has never actually been used as a unit of account.

But take note that Ether has already managed to entice worthwhile traction as a way to exchange goods and services and also to store value. Several Fortune 500 companies are now integrating Ethereum into their operations.

Moreover, the number of daily transactions have basically become more stable and increased since September 2015 according to the data released by EtherScan. The surge in transaction began in March

2016 with 23,362 daily transactions to an average of 428,007 as of this writing.

But even though this factor can help you make sense of how many individuals are using Ethereum today, this may not be the best criteria to look for because there is still a large percentage of DAO transactions that are generated through automated systems and does not actually reflect any economic activity. Instead, investors must find a way to determine which transactions are completed by actual people who are receiving or sending Ether from another user.

As Ether becomes more popular and many organizations are starting to focus on digital currencies, there will be a widespread acceptance on the digital currencies as a way to store value. The perception of Ether as a safe way to store value is a main driver of the digital currency's price.

The Role of Supply in Evaluating Ether

Unlike Bitcoin, which is capped at 21 million BTC, Ether has no supply cap. This makes another challenge for the investor to perform fundamental analysis and ascertain the role of supply.

In 2014, Ethereum launched a pre-sale of Ether, which has raised more than $14 Million. It was described as one of the largest crowdfunding efforts with some features of Initial Public Offering (IPO).

The donations collected from the pre-sale contributed to the initial supply as well as the rate of issuance today. Early investors received 60 million ETH, while 12 million ETH were allocated to the development fund, with the most percentage paid to the early contributors and developers.

These figures added up to the early supply of ETH which accounts to 72 million. In addition, the protocol of Ethereum allowed the creation of 5 ETH for each block mined. Also, a maximum of 18 million ETH were allowed to be created each year.

Financial analysts thus regard Bitcoin as gold (because of its supply cap) and Ethereum as dollars (because of its unlimited supply). Hence, fundamental analysis revolving on Ether supply can be akin to evaluating fiat currency.

Monitoring the Trends

Like in the forex and the stock market, the price of ETH can also be affected by what is happening in the world. For example, a primary currency exchange disrupted by a virus attack, or a state announcing a ban on digital currencies can affect the price of Ether, while companies accepting Ethereum or getting funded through ETH can influence the price to go up.

But analysts believe that relying on news for Ethereum investing is not a recommended main strategy. The main reason is that you may not have the luxury of the time to always hear the news first and react promptly. Usually, the market have already responded before you can even understand the whole scenario. You can use this as a supplemental investment strategy instead to confirm your market assumptions.

Some investors also capitalize on market corrections. More often than not, the market has the natural tendency to overreact to any news. They could panic sell without even understanding the full story. Therefore, a 20% decrease in ETH price, for example, is often followed by an increase between 5% and 10% as the market is adjusting to the hype. This is another way to use news reports for Ethereum investments.

Ethereum Swing Trading

So far, the strategies that we have explored are regarded as long-term investment strategies. They will take months or even years before they can provide you with substantial profits. There is always the risk of ending up with very minimal returns or even lose your capital.

If you want a faster way to make profits in Ethereum, you can try day trading, which is basically the method of buying or selling units on the basis of short-term fluctuations over the course of days or even minutes.

In the stocks and forex market, the most common strategy in day trading, which you can also use in cryptocurrencies such as Bitcoin and Ether is called swing trading. This is a method, which you can use to ascertain the turning points in the short-term trends.

You could make profits from the daily swings or the actual fluctuations in the ETH price whether the direction is downward or upward. In this strategy, you have to look for the support and resistance levels.

Resistance levels refers to the situation where an upward trend is projected to meet the resistance of sellers who are making profits. Support levels, on the other hand, refers to the downward movement of the price, which is expected to meet the resistance of buyers who are participating in the trade for a bargain.

Technical Analysis for Ethereum

In technical analysis, you need to use chart patterns and mathematical formula to predict the future movement of the ETH price. Unlike fundamental analysis, technical analysis is totally based on the past price movement and prediction of volume. Therefore, it does not cover any assumption if the price is too high or low. Rather, technical analysts believe that there are certain recurring patterns and trends, which will normally appear in any financial market.

Most of these patterns are dependent on human psychology based on the theory that participants in the markets are people who have the natural tendency to act in a particular way to various price movements. Some investors also suggest that the price fluctuations are affected by the behavior of the participants. Hence, understanding human behavior on risk and rewards can help you make a sound investment.

Technical analysis focuses more on the practical approach by assessing the history of the asset through price charts and using various analytical tools to make smart assumptions on how the market is feeling about Ethereum.

While fundamental analysis is more about estimating the value of the unit, technical analysis is more on keeping track of the actual price movement and predicting what will happen next. When you look at the price history of Ethereum, you can look at common trends such as support and resistance levels.

For better understanding of technical analysis, it is important to be familiar with the basic concepts of the Dow Theory, which is used as a standard in analyzing equities and currencies.

Here are Dow Theory's fundamental assumptions:

1. **History tend to repeat itself** - By understanding basic human psychology, you may be able to project the movement of the market, and so you could respond accordingly based on what happened in the past. For example, digital currencies like Bitcoin and Ether have regularly demonstrated bullish movements after significant events like announcements supporting these platforms.

2. **The price fluctuations are not completely random** - Instead, they follow trends that could be either short-term or long-term. If a unit is following a trend, there is a high chance that this will continue then go against it. Through technical analysis, you may identify Ethereum trends and make some profit from the price difference if you are interested in trading.

3. **Focus on the prevailing demand and supply** - In technical analysis, you have to

focus more on the track record of a unit and not more so on the specific factors that have caused the fluctuation. Even though there are several factors that you should also consider, believers of technical analysis normally take a more direct approach by assessing the current supply and demand.

4. **The market will discount past events** - Take note that all past, present, and even future assumptions are already factored in the existing price of a unit. For Ether, this also includes past, present, and future demand alongside the present regulations that are affecting digital currencies. The current price already reflects all the present information that also includes the information and expectation of market participants. Therefore, you should also consider what the price is signifying about the market mood, so you could make smarter predictions about price movements.

Evaluating Ethereum Trends

Taking a closer look on the general movement of Ether can help you make a sound investment in digital currencies. However, it can be a challenge to isolate these trends for analysis. Digital currencies are now very volatile, and assessing a chart of the price fluctuations of Ether usually reveals a series of rise and falls.

But using technical analysis, you could look past the volatility and identify the uptrend when you see a series of extreme falls and rises. By contrast, it is possible to isolate a downward trend when you identify a sequence of highs and lows. Apart from this, you may also need to consider sideway trends, in which the unit may demonstrate upward or downward trend. Take note that trends normally come in various lengths such as short-term, mid-term, and long-term.

The Buy & Hold Strategy

The other trading strategy is The Buy and Hold Ether Trading Strategy. It recognizes the loads of potential in Ether tokens, as well as in cryptocurrencies, in general. This strategy is very straightforward, and as its name suggests, it simply requires you to "buy" Ether tokens and "hold" these Ether tokens for a long period.

This strategy, also called *The Cold Storage Strategy*, is basically just acquiring a supply of Ether tokens, and then keeping the supply in a safe place. Examples of these safe places are hardware wallets and paper wallets.

Here are some advantages of the strategy:

- It can return high long-term capital gain; as proven, Ether tokens can be worth more in the long run. The idea is to stock up on Ether tokens, and then avoid touching them for at least 2 years. Once you open your account again, you can sell your Ether tokens, which could be priced much higher by then.

- It grants a profitable opportunity to people with no knowledge of complex financial terms and trading background. It does not require you to learn a month's worth of lessons about charts, technical and fundamental analyses, and other trading essentials.

On the other hand, while it comes with a set of advantages, The Buy and Hold Strategy also comes with a set of disadvantages. Here are some of them:

- It is a time-sensitive strategy. And as one, it necessitates a time investment of years.
- It ties up capital. Since it is a long-term strategy, it does not allow you to pursue other profitable opportunities with your capital. And unfortunately, it does not come with a 100% guarantee that your capital will multiply.

Chapter 7 - Step 3: Setup Your Account

While it isn't a walk in the park, investing in Ether and Ethereum isn't too complex. An interested individual (even a non-specialist) simply needs sufficient funds – preferably ones that are reserved just for ETH. Alongside, he needs to follow a few steps.

A Wallet

First off, an interested ETH investor needs to open an account in an Ethereum wallet. Doing so will allow him authority over Ether; apart from being able to store Ether, it will allow him to send and accept Ether payments.

Once an Ethereum wallet has been chosen, it's recommended to create an excellent first password – a strong one. Otherwise, it can be easily hacked.

Especially if you plan to store a lot of Ethers in your wallet, it's best to protect your wallet's privacy.

A strategy is to use a special hashing algorithm, which allows time-based password generation (i.e. it comes with a 30-second password generation feature). This doubles the security of the existing password and creates it in a more complex form.

Beyond protecting your password, other tips regarding the safety of Ethereum wallets are:

- You should protect your wallet's private keys. It's advisable to keep these keys private (i.e. not share with random individuals).
- You should not keep your ETH savings in a web-based wallet to minimize possible losses.

Since Ethereum is a decentralized platform, there is no authority that can facilitate the return of lost/stolen funds. So, if they get lost/stolen, chances are, Ethers will not be recovered.

- You should keep separate ETH wallets for different purposes. After all, an individual is allowed an unlimited number of wallets. For example, you should have an ETH wallet for your savings and another for your usual expenditures.

Factors to Consider When Choosing Wallets

It's important to choose the right kind of Ethereum wallet since there are both advantages and disadvantages to the different types out there. The different kinds of wallets are *web-based wallets, desktop wallets, hardware wallets, and mobile wallets.*

Features of web-based wallets:
- Authorized by 3rd party sources
- Linkable to desktop and mobile wallets
- Allows online storage of private keys

Features of desktop wallets:

- Features attractive user interface
- Supports multiple cryptocurrencies
- Supports multiple platforms
- Allows email recovery and restoration of funds

Features of hardware wallets:

- Features easy-to-navigate user interface
- Supports multiple cryptocurrencies
- Compact storage; keeps all Ether tokens in a single place
- Allows offline storage of private keys
- Impossible to hack online
- Difficult to hack when offline
- Durable
- Water-resistant
- Allows email recovery and restoration of funds when device is lost/stolen

Features of mobile wallets:

- Usable with NFC (or Near Field Communication) technology
- Supports multiple cryptocurrencies

- Allows easy accessibility of public and private keys; keys do not leave mobile devices

Creating Paper Wallets

You can also create paper wallets especially if you're an old-fashioned investor. While you can accidentally lose them, these paper wallets can be very secure for long-term storage. They are impossible to hack and are not susceptible to computer-related failures.

Features of paper wallets:

- Allows public and private keys to be printed on paper
- Considered popular and relatively secure
- Allows storage in safe locations (e.g. trusted financial institution and safety deposit box)

Here is a simple 3-step guide on how to create paper wallets:

- Step 1: First, buy a specific laser printer: one with small memory capacity and without fancy features (e.g. Wi-Fi connectivity, inkjet)
- Step 2: Next, buy waterproof and tear-proof paper.
- Step 3: Finally, create your wallet via an online wallet generator. To do this, you would need to go online and generate a first address. Then, after disconnecting from the net, generate a second address for printing. This second address is your official wallet's address.

Remember to protect your private key well. You a set of tamper-evident seals for safety precautions: to know whether somebody has been peeking at the private key.

Top Ethereum Wallets

The official wallet for Ethereum users is *Mist*.

Here is a 4-step guide on how to use Mist:

- Step 1: First, download Mist and select **Ethereum-Wallet-Your-System**. Make sure you're actually downloading the latest version. Alongside, make sure you download the release that meets your system requirements.
- Step 2: Next, launch Mist and wait for the node to sync.
- Step 3: Next (and once the Ethereum node is 100% synced), you will be prompted to select a network. Your choices are:
  - ○ **Use the Test Network** – this option allows the testing of the Mist application freely (without using actual Ether tokens) in a test network

○ **Use the Main Network** – this
option requires actual Ether tokens
for the execution of contracts
- Step 3: Next, you will be prompted to create
a password.
- Step 4: Finally, you will be redirected to your
account's dashboard. There, you will see the
amount of Ether tokens that you own, as
well as the Ethereum node's sync status.

Exchanges: Not Recommended as Wallets

While they may offer support for Ethereum, some
digital currency exchanges (e.g. CEX.io,
shapeshift.io, poloniex, Kraken, and BitPanda) are
not recommended to be used as wallets. Sure, if you
use these exchanges, it can be convenient to leave
and store your Ether tokens in their platform.

However, the primary nature of exchanges is to be a portal for cryptocurrency traders. Their services focuses on facilitating fair exchanges. And unfortunately, keeping your Ether tokens safe is not their priority.

Account Funding

After setting up an Ethereum wallet, funding your account is the next step. You will need a supply of Ether tokens, which you can buy via cash, credit card, or other payment methods.

Buying Ether Tokens via Wallets

For the following discussion, the official Ethereum wallet, Mist, will be used. As mentioned, it is your prerogative to use other Ethereum wallets. And since Ethereum wallets adhere to similar concepts, you may use the following instructions as reference.

Here is a -step guide on how to buy Ether tokens via wallets:

- Step 1: First, launch Mist and navigate your way to the Etherbase, which serves as your main account.
- Step 2: Next, locate the **Deposit Ether** section on the upper right side of the Etherbase.
- Step 3: Finally, enter the details for your preferred payment method.

Buying Ether Tokens via Exchanges

You can also choose to fund your account by buying Ether tokens via exchanges.

For the following example, an exchange that caters to worldwide customers, CEX.io will be used. Note that the fees for ETH on the exchange are calculated into the rate, which is why the fees may seem relatively high.

Here is a 5-step guide on how to buy Ether tokens via exchanges:

- Step 1: First, open an account on CEX.io.
- Step 2: Next, click on the **Deposit** tab. There, enter the details of your bank account, credit card, or preferred payment method.
- Step 3: Next, navigate your way to the **Buy/Sell** section.
- Step 4: Next, choose Ethereum and specify the number of Ether tokens you want to buy.
- Step 5: Finally (and once you double-check your entry regarding the number of Ether tokens you want to buy), click **Buy Ethereum**.

Account Funding by Investing in Ethereum CFDs

Apart from the conventional (and popular) means of funding your account, you can invest in *Ethereum CFDs (or Contract for Differences)*.

The idea behind these CFDs is that as an alternative to buying actual Ether tokens, you can trade Ether tokens according to an exchange rate. While this can put you on a major financial risk if you're an inexperienced trader, investing in Ethereum CFDs can also be very lucrative.

Account Funding by Mining

You can also fund your account by mining Ether tokens. Since it uses a PoW blockchain and involves diminishing block rewards, it is similar to mining Bitcoins. When mining Ether tokens, it is best to use dedicated GPUs.

Chapter 8 - Step 4: Diversify Your Digital Currency Investments

Even though you are investing in Ethereum - a new platform for storing value, this classic investment strategy still applies – diversification reigns supreme. It is of utmost importance to learn how to diversify your investments in digital currencies.

And even if you want to focus your investments in cryptocurrencies, you should diversify your investments by buying and holding different digital currencies that are now demonstrating a great deal of potential.

By diversifying your investments in digital currencies, you will be able to maximize your returns in various areas that will each react differently to the same event. Although this will not guarantee you against any loss, diversifying your investment will ensure that you will stay in the game despite of what may happen in the financial markets.

In this Chapter, you will get to know other three virtual currencies other than Bitcoin and Ether.

Litecoin (LTC)

LiteCoin is a virtual currency that also uses similar blockchain technology to Bitcoin and Ethereum. This was created by Charlie Lee - a former Google engineer who built this virtual currency as an open-source payment platform. Like Ethereum and Bitcoin, it is also free from any governance from a single entity. But Litecoin is different from Ethereum in areas like using scrypt as a proof of work system, and it also provides faster block generation.

Basically, LTC is designed as a lower-scale digital currency and developed with the objective of resolving the issues in Bitcoin technology. Litecoin is now a promising investment unit because it has already achieved peak liquidity and volume.

It is also interesting to take note that mining LTC is as fast as mining Ether. As such, it has rapidly became one of the top digital currencies in the world today in terms of value. This is also easier to mine compared to Bitcoin and Ether.

LTC supply is fixed at 84 million and the current value of 1 LTC in USD is $ 47.31, which can increase a lot in the years to come.

Ripple (XRP)

Ripple was introduced in 2012 as a global settlement network that offers low-cost international payments. This virtual cash allows banks to fulfill overseas payments in real-time with total transparency and affordable rates. XRP is considered as one of the most valuable cryptocurrencies today with its market capitalization around $1.26 billion.

Like Ethereum, XRP also runs on blockchain technology, called the consensus ledger, which acts as a way for confirming transactions. But this digital currency does not require mining, hence there is no need for network latency and computational power. The creators of XRP believes that the distribution of value is a better way to incentivize particular behaviors. Hence, XRP traders are distributing the currency through business deals, payments, and rewards.

Although XRP was introduced to the public in 2012, XRP was actually first created earlier than Ethereum. Ryan Fugger first worked on the project in 2004 as a decentralized cash system that can easily empower businesses and individuals to create their own storage of value.

In essence, XRP is a certificate of indebtedness, and the transactions are basically composed of balances that are being transmitted on a sequence of virtual cash reserves from one user to the other. As of this writing, the total volume of XRP in the market is valued around $500 million and the value of XRP / USD is 0.21021. This means that this digital currency has a lot of space for growth.

Zcash (ZEC)

Zcash is basically one of the newest open-source digital currency that was introduced only in late 2016, but it has already caught the attention of many investors and traders.

Basically, Zcash positions itself as a more secured form of digital currency. It offers privacy as well as selective transaction transparency. Hence, it is often referenced to as the https of the digital currencies, because it offers extra privacy or security where all transactions will appear in the public ledger, but the details will remain hidden.

Zcash also provides its users the option for shielded transactions that will allow your content to be encrypted through advanced cryptographic strategies or zero-knowledge proof known as the zk-SNARK.

As of this writing, the market volume of ZEC is around $68 million and its price is $264.21.

Conclusion

Thank you for taking the time to read this book!

You should now have a good understanding of Ethereum and decide if this is really a good instrument to invest your money or make profits through trading.

CPSIA information can be obtained
at www.ICGtesting.com
Printed in the USA
LVHW051453300321
682937LV00020B/1540